D0903178

Rolling in the Aisles

A Collection of Laugh-Out-Loud Poems

Rolling in the Aisles
A Collection of Laugh-Out-Loud Poems

Edited by **Bruce Lansky**
Illustrated by **Stephen Carpenter**

𝑚 Meadowbrook Press

Distributed by Simon & Schuster
New York

Library of Congress Cataloging-in-Publication Data

Rolling in the aisles : a collection of laugh-out-loud poems / edited by Bruce Lansky ; illustrated by Stephen Carpenter.
    p. cm.
  Includes index.
  ISBN 0-88166-473-1 (Meadowbrook) ISBN 0-689-03766-X (Simon & Schuster)
  1. Children's poetry, American. 2. Humorous poetry, American. I. Lansky, Bruce. II. Carpenter, Stephen, ill.
  PS586.3.R65 2004
  811'.07089282—dc22
                        2004005295

Editorial Director: Christine Zuchora-Walske
Coordinating Editor and Copyeditor: Angela Wiechmann
Proofreader: Joseph Gredler
Production Manager: Paul Woods
Graphic Design Manager: Tamara Peterson

© 2004 by Meadowbrook Creations

All rights reserved. No part of this book may be reproduced or transmitted in any form or by any means, electronic or mechanical, including photocopying, recording, or using any information storage and retrieval system, without written permission from the publisher, except in the case of brief quotations embodied in critical articles and reviews.

Published by Meadowbrook Press, 5451 Smetana Drive, Minnetonka, Minnesota 55343

www.meadowbrookpress.com

BOOK TRADE DISTRIBUTION by Simon and Schuster, a division of Simon and Schuster, Inc., 1230 Avenue of the Americas, New York, New York 10020

09 08 07 06 05 04   10 9 8 7 6 5 4 3 2 1

Printed in the United States of America

Dedication

To all the kids who tested
the poems in this book and the
teachers who made that possible.

To all the kids who visit GigglePoetry.com to
read poetry, have fun with poetry, learn how to write
poetry, and submit their poems for online publication.
(Tell your teachers about PoetryTeachers.com.)

To all the teachers who visit PoetryTeachers.com
to learn how to teach poetry, make poetry fun,
and find poets they can invite to their schools.
(Tell your students about GigglePoetry.com.)

Acknowledgments

Many thanks to the following teachers and their students who tested poems during the six years we've worked on this anthology:

Marcy Anderson, Dell Rapids Elementary, Dell Rapids, SD
Kate Arthurs, St. Martin's Episcopal School, Metairie, LA
Patty Bachman, Rockford, IL
Karen Benson, Highland Elementary School, Apple Valley, MN
Mark Benthall, Lakeway Elementary, Austin, TX
Gayle Billings, Happy Valley Primary, Anderson, CA
Kathy Budahl, L. B. Williams Elementary, Mitchell, SD
Nicole Cantin, Hawley Elementary, Hawley, MN
Monica Chun, Edgewood School, Woodridge, IL
Diane Clapp, Lincoln Elementary, Faribault, MN
Connie Cooper, Lincoln Elementary, Faribault, MN
Bonnie Cox, Kolmar School, Midlothian, IL
Diane Czajak, McCarthy Elementary, Framingham, MA
Helen Dawkins, Lakeway Elementary, Austin, TX
Cheryl Esparza, Monroe School, Hinsdale, IL
Richard Forrest, East Elementary, New Richmond, WI
Marianne Gately, McCarthy Elementary, Framingham, MA
Pamela Greer, East Elementary, New Richmond, WI
Nancy Hausman, Medary Elementary, Brookings, SD
Rita Hawley, West Elementary, New Richmond, WI
Kathy Hayes, Skyline Elementary, Elkhorn, NE
Shirl Herzig, Groveland Elementary, Wayzata, MN
Jane Hesslein, Sunset Hill Elementary, Plymouth, MN
Kate Hooper, Island Lake Elementary, Shoreview, MN
Lori Horstmeyer, Dell Rapids Elementary, Dell Rapids, SD
Leslie James, Cottonwood, CA
Janet Jobes, Knickrehm Elementary, Grand Island, NE
Ann Johnson, McAuliffe Elementary, Hastings, MN
Sandra Kane, Lincoln Elementary, Faribault, MN
Margaret Kelberer, St. Paul Academy, St. Paul, MN
Kathy Kenney-Marshall, McCarthy Elementary, Framingham, MA
Sharon Klein, Clardy Elementary, Kansas City, MO
Barbara Knoss, Hanover School, Hanover, MN
Maggie Knutson, Orono Intermediate School, North Long Lake, MN

Mike Koenig, Rum River Elementary, Andover, MN
Carolyn Larsen, Rum River Elementary, Andover, MN
Carol Larson, Rum River Elementary, Andover, MN
Adrianne Lemberg, Hudson, WI
Carmen Markgren, East Elementary, New Richmond, WI
Patricia Marshall, Minneapolis, MN
Kathleen McMahon, McCarthy Elementary, Framingham, MA
Julie Meissner, Turtle Bay School, Redding, CA
Loralu Meyer, Southview Elementary, Apple Valley, MN
Karen Mink, Edgewood School, Woodridge, IL
Jenny Myer, East Elementary, New Richmond, WI
Elaine Nick, Gracemor Elementary, Kansas City, MO
Mary Niermann, Lincoln Elementary, Faribault, MN
Tessie Oconer, Fulton Elementary, Minneapolis, MN
Eric Ode, Stewart Elementary, Puyallup, WA
James Parr, McCarthy Elementary, Framingham, MA
Connie Parrish, Gertie Bell Rodgers Elementary, Mitchell, SD
Robert Pottle, Cave Hill School, Eastbrook, ME
John Pundsack, East Elementary, New Richmond, WI
Ruth Refsnider, East Elementary, New Richmond, WI
Cathy Rodrigue, Deer Creek Elementary, Crowley, TX
Connie Roetzer, East Elementary, New Richmond, WI
Andrea Rutkowski, Miscoe Hill School, Mendon, MA
Sheila Sandell, Taylors Falls Elementary, Taylors Falls, MN
M. J. Savaiano, Museum Magnet School, St. Paul, MN
Beverly Semanko, Rum River Elementary, Andover, MN
Maria Smith, Deer Creek Elementary, Crowley, TX
Will and Mary Snyder, Fall River Mills, CA
Christy Strayhorn, Deer Creek Elementary, Crowley, TX
Carleen Tjader, East Elementary, New Richmond, WI
Tim Tocher, George Grant Mason Elementary, Tuxedo, NY
Carolyn D. Wanek, St. Martin's Episcopal School, Metairie, LA
Jory Westberry, Golden Gate Elementary, Naples, FL
Margie Thell Weiss, East Elementary, New Richmond, WI
Julie White, East Elementary, New Richmond, WI
Sue Wiechmann, Riverside Elementary, Brainerd, MN
DeLinda Youngblood, Centralia, IL.

Contents

Introduction

I don't know if it's accurate to state that *Rolling in the Aisles* is the funniest poetry anthology we've ever published. (It has some very stiff competition for that honor.) But I'm pretty sure it's the best written. I started scouting for funny poems to include in *Rolling in the Aisles* six years ago (right after *Miles of Smiles* was published). Over the last few years, we've tested hundreds of poems with a huge panel of almost six thousand elementary- and middle-school children. I'm very happy to present to you the result of all that hard work.

When I first started collecting funny poems for anthologies years ago, there was a very small number of "famous" children's poets. At the time, I was in an equally small group of up-and-coming poets. Since then, the multimillion-copy success of my anthologies—*Kids Pick the Funniest Poems*, *A Bad Case of the Giggles*, *Miles of Smiles*, and *No More Homework! No More Tests!*—has generated great interest in humorous poetry among kids, parents, teachers, and writers. The popularity of GigglePoetry.com, the number one children's poetry website, has also motivated hundreds of poets to submit poetry for possible inclusion in our anthologies.

Today, the group of "famous" poets is still a small one. In the last few years, that group has been diminished by the loss of Shel Silverstein and Jeff Moss—two of my all-time favorites. But the number of rising stars seems to be multiplying. This book contains poems by poets whose talent I'd like to highlight: Kenn Nesbitt, Ted Scheu, Linda Knaus, Neal Levin, Robert Pottle, Kathy Kenny-Marshall, Dave Crawley, Eric Ode, Darren Sardelli, Mark Benthall, Diane Z. Shore, and Helen Ksypka (whose name I can't pronounce properly, which is the only reason I listed her last). I'm happy to report that many of these folks visit schools, and you can learn more about them on PoetryTeachers.com (a website for teachers looking for ideas on how to make poetry more fun for their students).

I still enjoy reading poems in the hope of finding some I think you'd enjoy. I'd like to thank editor Angie Wiechmann for reading thousands of poems so I can focus my attention on the ones most likely to appeal to you. I hope you enjoy the fruits of our happy labor.

Bruce Lansky

Home
on the
Range

My Normal Family

My daddy snores and sucks his toes.
My brother likes to lick his nose.
My doggy meows, my kitten barks.
My goldfish chases sticks in parks.
My sister walks while upside down.
My mother hops all over town.
Her skin is purple, don't you know.
And I am green from head to toe.
My dad is red, my sister's blue.
My brother's yellow; yes, it's true.
We all wear raincoats in the sun
And gobble lima beans for fun.
We're very special, can't you see?
We're just a normal family!

Kathy Kenney-Marshall

3

Meat Loaf

My mother made a meat loaf,
but I think she made it wrong.
**It could be that she cooked
it**
just a little bit too long.

She pulled it from the oven,
and we all began to choke.
The meat loaf was on fire,
and the kitchen filled with smoke.

The smoke detectors squealed
from all the flaming meat loaf haze.
My father used his drink
to try extinguishing the blaze.

Mom shrieked and dropped the meat loaf;
it exploded with a boom
and splattered blackened globs on
every surface in the room.

The dog passed out. The kitten hid.
My brother screamed and fled.
The baby ate a gobbet
sticking to her head.

My father started yelling,
and my sister went berserk.
But I kept cool and said, "At least
our smoke detectors work."

Linda Knaus and Kenn Nesbitt

5

It Can't Be Time to Take a Bath

It can't be time to take a bath.
I took one just last week.
I'm sure the spots you think are grime
are freckles on my cheek.

I'm just as clean as clean can be.
You won't find any dirt.
I rubbed my mouth clean with my hands,
then wiped them on my shirt.

My feet were muddy yesterday,
but that's no longer true.
I walked home barefoot in the rain,
so now they're spotless, too.

There was some gunk behind my ears—
a funny shade of gray.
Don't worry, though, 'cause it's all gone.
The cat licked it away.

And so you see, there is no need
to point me toward the tub.
It's just a waste of water.
I've got nothing left to scrub!

A. Maria Plover

6

Now I Lay Me Down to Rest

Soon I'll lay me down to rest,
but first I have to get undressed,
comb the tangles from my hair,
change my dirty underwear,
have a sandwich and a drink,
clean the plate and rinse the sink,
feed the goldfish, take a bath,
do my spelling and my math,
check my head for ticks and lice,
leave some cheese out for the mice,
fold and put away my pants,
sing a song and do a dance,
say goodnight to Dad and Mother,
pick a fight with my twin brother,

blow my nose and set the clock,
take the dog out for a walk,
turn the light out, pull the shade,
have a glass of lemonade,
trim my toenails, clean my ears,
eat a jar of pickle spears,
kiss Aunt May and Uncle Keith,
wash my face and brush my teeth,
take the garbage to the curb,
learn a pronoun from a verb
so I can pass tomorrow's test—
but now I'm too awake to rest.

Linda Knaus

Mind Your Manners

Don't drum on the table.
Don't play with your food.
Don't talk while you're chewing;
it's terribly rude.

Don't leave the fridge open.
Don't slam the screen door.
Don't throw dirty laundry
all over the floor.

Don't fight with your brother.
Don't pull the cat's tail.
Don't open your big sister's
personal mail.

Don't pester your parents.
Don't stick out your tongue.
Don't do what your parents did
when they were young.

Bruce Lansky

9

I Bought My Mom an Apple

I bought my mom an apple,
but it wasn't red or green;
it was kind of bluish purple
or some color in between.

I wouldn't call the blueberries
I bought her very blue;
they were more like reddish orange
with a light vermilion hue.

The oranges I got for her
weren't orange as you'd think;
they were yellow on the inside
and the orange peels were pink.

The strawberries I purchased
weren't particularly red;
they were white with purple polka dots
and yellow stripes instead.

I got all these by shopping
where I'd never shopped before.
That's the last time I buy groceries
at the Rainbow grocery store!

Kenn Nesbitt

Mommy's Jewelry

I wear my mommy's bracelets.
I put on all her rings.
I always love the way I look
in Mommy's sparkly things.

I wear her favorite necklace.
It's made of solid gold.
It's filled with gems and precious stones.
It's trendy and it's bold.

I pin all Mommy's brooches
in line across my shirt.
I handle each one carefully
and try not to get hurt.

I reach for Mommy's earrings,
then Mom walks though the door.
She looks upset to find me dressed
in jewels and gold galore.

"I told you not to do this!"
My mommy has a cow.
"You mustn't wear my jewelry—
John, take it off right now!"

Angela Magnan

11

Vac

Our vacuum cleaner has
Sucked up the cat
The morning paper
The kitchen mat
Two dozen spiders
A pair of shoes
A vest and panties
(I'm not sure whose)
Some CDs and
Cassettes galore
A nest of tables
The bathroom door
The electric cooker
The TV set
An ancient picture
Of my first pet
Our neighbor's dog
The mailman, too
Our dining chairs
My father's shoe
Some plastic bricks—
And what a drag!
I think I need to
Change the bag.

Trevor Harvey

Everything's Relative

Fraidy Cat

Every night he wakes me up,
all crying and upset.
He thinks he heard a monster,
and now his bed is wet.

"I heard a noise, and now I'm scared,"
he says through all the tears.
I wipe his face and pat his head
and hug away his fears.

I check for ghosts inside his room
and look behind the door.
I scare off all the bogeymen
and tell him, "Cry no more."

I understand his fear of ghosts.
It wouldn't be so bad,
but it's really kind of silly—
this fraidy cat's my dad.

Matthew M. Fredericks

14

Daddy's Nails

Last night while Daddy slept
I started polishing his nails.
I knew just what they needed.
My solution never fails.

A few I colored purple
And a few fluorescent pink.
The rest were hot magenta
And a couple black, I think.

He showed them off to Mommy.
She admired all the gloss.
At work he showed his buddies
And especially his boss.

My Daddy's nails are lovely—
All those colors, all those hues.
Tomorrow I'll start polishing
His hammers and his screws.

Neal Levin

15

Daddy's Making Dinner

Daddy's making dinner
I've seen it all before
French fries black and burning
And meat loaf on the floor

Daddy's making dinner
The sugar bowl just broke
Fido ate the gravy
The house has filled with smoke

Daddy's making dinner
But I'm not one to moan
Soon he will surrender
And go pick up the phone

Daddy made the dinner
Today's my lucky day
Dinner's in the trash can
And pizza's on the way

Jeff Mondak

What I'd Like to Ask My Grandma

When I sit on your knee, Gran,
I can see right up your nose.
You must be really old, Gran,
To grow hairs as long as those.

You must be really old, Gran,
To have wrinkles on your chin.
I find it hard to tell, Gran,
Where your chin and neck begin.

I have a tooth that's wobbly,
So before I'm eighty-two,
Will I take all my teeth out
Like you and Grandad do?

Trevor Harvey

Uncle Alfonso's Hair

Uncle Alfonso has hair on his toes,
and under his armpits it plentif'ly flows.

It juts from his fingers and out of his ears.
The tops of his shoulders are needy of shears.

There's bunches and bunches that sprout from his back.
His chest and his stomach of hair do not lack.

It's all over his legs and inside his nose,
but his head is the one place his hair never grows.

Helen Ksypka

Brothers
and
Sisters

My Brother's Bear

My baby brother has a bear
that travels with him everywhere.
He never lets the bear from sight.
He hugs it in his crib at night.

And when my brother's diaper smells,
the name of the bear is what he yells.
Which is a clever thing to do
because my brother named him Pooh.

Bruce Lansky

My Brother Fred

I'd like to introduce you
    to my little brother, Fred.
He doesn't walk or talk yet;
    there's just peach fuzz on his head.

He never plays computer games
    or listens to CDs.
I can't get him to watch TV;
    he's really hard to please.

One day I made him pizza,
    but he spit it out and cried.
The only foods he ever eats
    are strained or liquefied.

He yells and hollers every night,
    so I can't get to sleep.
But when I'm up and dressed for school
    he doesn't make a peep.

He's always leaking, so it seems,
    from one end or the other.
If I could get my way, I'd trade him
    for an older brother.

My mom said he's a baby
    and that's what babies do.
I wish she'd found one broken in
    instead of one brand-new.

A. Maria Plover

Baby Ate a Microchip

Baby ate a microchip,
Then grabbed a bottle, took a sip.
He swallowed it and made a beep,
And now he's thinking pretty deep.

He's downloading his ABCs
And calculating 1-2-3s.
He's memorizing useless facts
While doing Daddy's income tax.

He's processing, and now he thrives
On feeding his internal drives.
He's throwing fits, and now he fights
With ruthless bits and toothless bytes.

He must be feeling very smug.
But hold on, Baby caught a bug.
Attempting to reboot in haste,
He accidentally got erased!

Neal Levin

23

My Brother Bart

My brother Bart is such a dunce.
He hadn't changed his socks in months.
He hadn't changed his underwear
in just about a year, I swear.
Though they were always caked with dirt,
He never changed his pants and shirt.
All were shocked and horrified
that Bart could find no place to hide
when at the stroke of noon today,
his clothes got up and walked away.

Linda Knaus

Oh, Brother!

My brother has such stinky feet;
He's a naughty little kid.
When Mama asked him if he bathed,
He lied and said he did.

He wears his T-shirts inside out
And doesn't seem to care.
His clothes don't match, his face unclean,
A comb can't part his hair.

He stuffed my shoes with toilet paper,
Hid my favorite dolls,
Put bugs inside my dresser drawers,
Left handprints on my walls.

He scribbled on my homework
And made faces at my friend,
Stuck his tongue out—then he laughed!
(Oh, will this ever end?)

Then yesterday my mama said:
"I know how you love your brother.
You'll be happy to hear in a few short months
You're going to have another!"

Nancy Jean Clemens

25

Favorite Feature

My brother Melvin stares into the mirror every night.
He loves the way his left eye matches nicely with his right.

He's discovered there are moments when he has to hold back tears
While he marvels at the absolute perfection of his ears.

He's decided that his eyebrows make him look extremely wise.
And how clever he must be for having one for both his eyes.

He's convinced that if his lips were gone he'd really, really miss them.
So he brings the mirror close enough to pucker up and kiss them.

Melvin's fascination with his features grows and grows.
But when asked which one he likes the best, he always picks his nose.

Linda Knaus

Not True

Do you know what my brother did?
He pushed me down, then ran and hid!

He pinched me purple, poked my eye.
He kicked my rear and made me cry.

He hit me with a pillow—hard—
then chased me all around the yard.

He opened up my private mail
then said I was a tattletale.

And since that simply is not true,
that's why I had to come tell you.

Ann Dorer

Lost and Found

This morning, Mom reminded me
to check the Lost and Found.
So just to make her happy,
I took a look around.

The box was like a stinky mouth,
whose grin was dark and wide.
I gulped and took a monster breath
then reached my arm inside.

I dug around without a sound
through swirls of clothes and dirt.
To my delight, the box spit out
my favorite soccer shirt.

I peered a little deeper down,
and there, to my surprise,
a little face gazed up at me
with wide and eager eyes.

I took a triple-double take
and saw it was my sister.
It's sad to think—for several weeks,
we hadn't even missed her.

Ted Scheu

Magic Show

I'm going to a magic show.
There is a trick I hope they know.
So I'll go with my sister dear
and hope they make her disappear.

Robert Pottle

Friends

Love Struck

Cupid is stupid!
Look what he's done!
He's made the girls like us
And ruined our fun.
Before, we could chase them
And cause them to fuss.
But since Cupid got them,
The girls all chase us.

Amy S. Mullins

Foul Mouth

Oh my goodness!
Oh my gosh!
Eddie's going
Through the wash!

His dirty mouth's
So mad and mean.
Maybe this
Will get it clean!

While we wait
And watch
And hope. . .
I'll pour in some
    extra soap!

Ted Scheu

33

I Like You (Not)

I like you lots. (That isn't true.)
I like most everything you do.
I like that lovely smile you make.
(I think it's phony—I think you're fake.)
I like the light upon your face.
(When it's bright, it's a disgrace.)
I like to watch you eat your food.
(The way you chew, it's just so rude.)
I truly like your tone of voice.
(I'd turn it off if I had the choice.)
I absolutely love your walk.
(I wish you'd do it off the dock.)
I like the way you keep your hair.
(What is with that goofy stare?)
I like you lots. I think you're cool!
(Because it's hot...and you own a pool.)

Dan Wilson

My First Best Friend

My first best friend is Awful Ann—
she socked me in the eye.
My second best is Sneaky Sam—
he tried to swipe my pie.
My third best friend is Max the Rat—
he trampled on my toes.
My fourth best friend is Nasty Nell—
she almost broke my nose.

My fifth best friend is Ted the Toad—
he kicked me in the knee.
My sixth best friend is Grumpy Gail—
she's always mean to me.
My seventh best is Monster Moe—
he often plays too rough.
That's all the friends I've got right now—
I think I've got enough.

Jack Prelutsky

Pets

My Dog Has Got No Manners

My dog has got no manners.
I think he's very rude.
He always whines at dinnertime
while we are eating food.

And when he's feeling thirsty
and wants to take a drink,
he takes it from the toilet
instead of from the sink.

He never wears a pair of pants.
He doesn't wear a shirt.
But worse, he will not shower
to wash away the dirt.

He's not polite to strangers.
He bites them on the rear.
And when I'm on the telephone,
he barks so I can't hear.

When I complained to Mommy,
she said, "I thought you knew.
The reason that his manners stink:
he learns by watching you."

Bruce Lansky

Dog Hollywood

I taught my dog to sit and heel and how to fetch a stick.
And then I taught him how to do a cool karate kick.

I taught him how to roll his eyes, pretending he was dead.
And how to dance a German polka standing on his head.

Of course I had to teach him how to speak in Japanese.
And juggle thirteen apricots while swinging through the trees.

A Hollywood producer saw him doing all his tricks.
My doggy signed a contract, and now he's making flicks.

I haven't heard from my old pooch since back in ninety-nine.
His agent's taking all his calls; I guess he's doing fine.

Now everybody wants to see him do his fancy shows.
How quickly he forgot the one who taught him all he knows.

Tom Shadley

My Dog Likes to Disco

My doggy likes to disco dance.
He boogies every night.
He dances in his doghouse
till the early morning light.

The other dogs come running
when they hear my doggy swing.
A few will play their instruments.
The others dance and sing.

They pair off with their partners
as their tails begin to wag.
They love to do the Bunny Hop,
the fox trot, and the shag.

You'll see the doghouse rockin'
as a hundred dogs or more
all trip the light fantastic
on the doghouse disco floor.

At last, at dawn they exit
in the early morning breeze,
and stop to sniff the fire hydrants,
bushes, lawns, and trees.

I just don't understand it,
for although it looks like fun,
I can't see how they fit inside
that doghouse built for one.

Kenn Nesbitt

The Favorite

My family got a brand-new dog,
A most attractive mutt.
I think that I'm her favorite 'cuz
She bit me on my butt.
She only licks my brother's face.
She only begs for Mom.
She only fetches for Aunt Kate
And "speaks" for Uncle Tom.
My sister doesn't stand a chance;
The dog sleeps in my bed.
And 'cuz there's only room for one,
I'm on the floor instead.
When I come home she knocks me down.
She growls and eats my shirts.
But since it's 'cuz she loves me lots,
It barely even hurts.
I know she loves me madly.
She adores me through and through.
I'm certain 'cuz just yesterday
She pooped inside my shoe.
Today I was her favorite 'cuz
She ate my scrambled eggs.
And then she chewed my brand-new shoes
And scratched me on my legs.
She likes to play with only me.
We play "prisoner" all day.
She makes me sit and growls
If I attempt to get away.
She plays another game with me:
She's "it" at hide-and-seek.
She "smiles" and shows her teeth when I
Give up or try to peek.
And though it's great to be so loved
And sometimes I have fun,
As she gets big it's scaring me
That I'm her favorite one.

Kathy Kenney-Marshall

Mirror, Mirror, o'er the Sink

"Mirror, mirror, o'er the sink,
Tell me what you really think.
Do my lovely eyes of brown
Dazzle like a diamond crown?
Is my hair of gleaming gold
Beautiful, as I am told?"

Quoth the mirror, "Yes, 'tis true.
All these things are said of you.
Still, I beg you, back away.
Clearly, you've not flossed today.
Kibble breath has made me fog.
Off the sink, you stupid dog!"

Kimberly Norman

43

Don't Forget to Share

The parakeets are laughing.
The fish are doing flips.
The cats and dogs are dancing
with ice cream on their lips.

The birds and mice are singing.
The snakes are having fun.
A turtle is enjoying
a hot dog on a bun.

The crabs are all delighted.
The toads are jumping high.
A monkey just devoured
a piece of pumpkin pie.

The pigs are eating apples.
The frogs are drinking punch.
It's nice to see them sharing
the pet shop owner's lunch.

Darren Sardelli

45

Cat and Mouse

The mouse, it's said,
finds cats ill-bred.
They make his stomach sicken.
My cat thinks mice
are rather nice
and taste a bit like chicken.

Eric Ode

46

My Goldfish

My goldfish died this morning
At exactly half past seven.

My mother helped me say a prayer,
Then flushed him into heaven.

Mark Benthall

Little Abigail and the Beautiful Pony

There was a girl named Abigail
Who was taking a drive
Through the country
With her parents
When suddenly she spied a beautiful
    sad-eyed
Grey and white pony.
And next to it was a sign
That said,
FOR SALE—CHEAP.
"Oh," said Abigail,
"May I have that pony?
May I please?"
And her parents said,
"No you may not."
And Abigail said,
"But I MUST have that pony."
And her parents said,
"Well, you can't have that pony,
But you can have a nice butter pecan
Ice cream cone when we get home."
And Abigail said,
"I don't want a butter pecan
Ice cream cone,
I WANT THAT PONY—
I MUST HAVE THAT PONY."

And her parents said,
"Be quiet and stop nagging—
You're *not* getting that pony."
And Abigail began to cry and said,
"If I don't get that pony I'll die."
And her parents said, "You won't die.
No child ever died yet from not
    getting a pony."
And Abigail felt so bad
That when they got home she went
    to bed,
And she couldn't eat,
And she couldn't sleep,
And her heart was broken,
And she DID die—
All because of a pony
That her parents wouldn't buy.

(This is a good story
To read to your folks
When they won't buy
You something you want.)

Shel Silverstein

48

School

Rules for the Bus

Said our driver in September
as we climbed aboard the bus,
"There are rules you must remember.
Number one, you do not cuss.
Do not squirm and do not wiggle.
Do not squeak and do not squawk.
Do not laugh and do not giggle.
Better yet, don't even talk.
Do not ever let me catch you
with your feet out in the aisle.
Sit as rigid as a statue
with a stiff and silent smile.
And you will not wear your mittens,
and you will not wear a mask.
And you will not bring your kittens,
and you shouldn't even ask.
And you will not play with bubbles
or a yo-yo or balloon.
And for causing me such troubles
you will get them back in June.

Now the day is here. Begin it
with the words I have to say.
Kindly take a seat this minute,
and let's have a pleasant day."
Well, I listened very closely
to the messages I heard,
and in all this time I've mostly
followed each and every word.
I have tried to pay attention,
but of this, I must confess:
There's a rule he didn't mention,
and today it caused a mess.
It is not as if I planned it
with an evil attitude.
I am not that underhanded,
and I don't mean to be crude.
But it causes quite a fuss,
and it might even be unlawful
to have climbed aboard the bus
when you have stepped in something awful.

Eric Ode

51

Afterschool Snack

Right now I'm kinda hungry, dude.
The 'frigerator's full of food.
There's meat loaf and a chicken wing
And half a turkey sandwich-thing.

There's day-old tuna, almost new,
Some Tupperware with potluck stew,
Some leftover spaghetti sauce,
And wilted salad partly tossed.

There's also Jell-O (sort of green),
A chunk of cheese, a lima bean,
A jar of pickles, can of soup,
And something best described as goop.

There's broccoli that's growing old,
A loaf of bread that's growing mold...
The 'frigerator's full, but hey—
There's nothing that I want today.

Neal Levin

Excuse Cheer

Our center's nose was runny. Our forwards had the flu.
The guards were feeling funny. That's why we lost to you.
Your team is overrated. We really didn't try.
Our coach was constipated. I'm telling you no lie.
Now go and take a shower and hop back on your bus.
You know we'll beat you next time, so you'd best watch out for us!

Timothy Tocher

Benjie Poffenroth

Little Benjie Poffenroth
Was such a sneaky kid;
He didn't want to go to school,
So here's what Benjie did:

He went and dumped a big ol' bowl
Of oatmeal on his face,
And let it dry until it formed
A crusty, gross disgrace.

It only took one look to nearly
Make his mom collapse.
She thought, "Oh no! My baby boy's
Got leprosy, perhaps."

The doctor took a careful look…
And then he took another.
He scraped a sample off the cheek
To show to Benjie's mother.

The doctor smiled and said that all
Her worries had been hasty.
He popped the sample in his mouth
And said, "It's rather tasty!"

"Yes, Benjie should return to school—
He's played a little trick."
But seeing what the doctor did
Made Benjie's mom get sick.

Christopher Cook

Open House

I brought my dad to open house.
I also brought my mom.
I brought my Auntie Kathy,
and I brought my Uncle Dom.
I invited Nana Betty.
I invited Papa Fred.
They brought my baby cousin,
who was sleeping in their bed.
I brought my cousins Joe and Jim.
They brought their nephew Phil,
who brought his mom and dad and cat
and German shepherd, Lil.
I also asked my neighbor George;
I've known him all my life.
He brought his son and daughter,
and he also brought his wife,
who thought it rude not to invite
our other neighbor, Bob,
who asked his niece Belinda
and her son (who's such a slob).
He brought along his teddy bear
whose name is Poochykin.
My classroom is so crowded now
my teacher can't fit in.

Kathy Kenney-Marshall

School Lunch

Our school lunch is from outer space,
Endangering the human race.
The meatballs bounce right off the floor.
The fish cakes could break down a door.
The bread was baked ten years ago.
The burgers look like they will grow.
The chicken has the chicken pox.
The peas are frozen in a box.
The spinach gives your legs gangrene.
The fruit juice tastes like gasoline.
The soup is salty as the sea.
The franks explode like TNT.
The salad bar—don't dare to try it.
The carrot cake once caused a riot.
The deadly tuna casserole
Can bore a hole right through the bowl.
The fries could knock you off your chair.
The corn could make you lose your hair.
The way they cook here is a crime,

But lunch is still my favorite time.

Douglas Florian

Sick, Sick, Sick

I Brushed My Teeth Each Morning

I brushed my teeth each morning.
I brushed my teeth each night.
I brushed my teeth each time I ate.
My dentist cheered, "All right!"

But then one day I said, "No way!
I'll brush my teeth no more."
I didn't brush for one whole week
And then for four weeks more.

And then for eight weeks after that
I did not brush a lick.
I started chewing bubble gum
And chewed stick after stick.

I kept it up for one whole year.
No brushing, like I said.
My dentist found no cavities—
My teeth fell out instead.

Judith Natelli McLaughlin

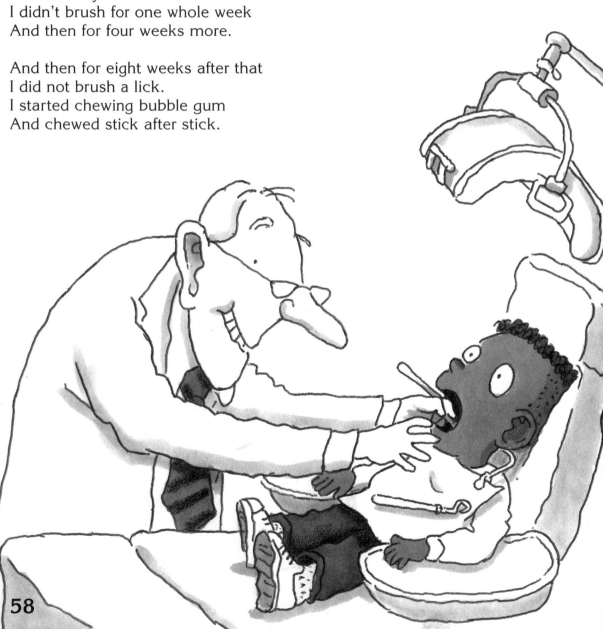

58

Curing the Hiccups

I have the...*hic, hic*...hiccups,
And nothing that's been done
Has helped at...*hic, hic*...curing them.
Hic, hic...This isn't fun.

I've breathed into their paper bags
And...*hic*...counted to ten.
I've...*hic*...been scared by everyone
And...*hic*...been scared again.

I've...*hic*...walked on a balance beam.
I've...*hic*...stood on my head.
I hope they cure them pretty soon
Before I'm...*hic, hic*...dead!

Mary Jane Mitchell

My Parents Are Pretending

I'm pretty sure my parents are
pretending they are sick.
I know because I taught them both
to do that little trick.

You blow your nose and hold your head
and claim your brain is breaking.
And so, a pro like me would know
my folks are clearly faking.

A little thing I learned in school
convinced me I am right.
My parents are supposed to meet
my principal tonight.

Ted Scheu

61

Willie's Wart

Willie had a stubborn wart
upon his middle toe.
Regardless, though, of what he tried
the wart refused to go.

So Willie went and visited
his family foot physician,
who instantly agreed
it was a stubborn wart condition.

The doctor tried to squeeze the wart.
He tried to twist and turn it.
He tried to scrape and shave the wart.
He tried to boil and burn it.

He poked it with a pair of tongs.
He pulled it with his tweezers.
He held it under heat lamps,
and he crammed it into freezers.

Regrettably these treatments
were of very little use.
He looked at it and sputtered,
"Ach! I cannot get it loose!"

"I'll have to get some bigger tools
to help me to dissect it.
I'll need to pound and pummel it,
bombard it and inject it."

He whacked it with a hammer,
and he yanked it with a wrench.
He seared it with a welding torch
despite the nasty stench.

He drilled it with a power drill.
He wrestled it with pliers.
He zapped it with a million volts
from large electric wires.

He blasted it with gamma rays,
besieged it with corrosives,
assaulted it with dynamite
and nuclear explosives.

He hit the wart with everything,
but when the smoke had cleared,
poor Willie's stubborn wart remained,
and Willie'd disappeared.

Linda Knaus and Kenn Nesbitt

Insomnia

I cannot get to sleep tonight.
I toss and turn and flop.
I try to count some fluffy sheep
while o'er a fence they hop.
I try to think of pleasant dreams
of places really cool.
I don't know why I cannot sleep—
I slept just fine at school.

Kathy Kenney-Marshall

Out and About

Spring Will Be Pretty

Spring will be pretty. Just give it a week,
When flowers are blooming down by the creek.
Bees will be buzzing as trees start to bud,
But for the moment I'm covered with mud.

Snow has been melting, since winter is through,
Replacing the whiteness with puddles of goo.
I stepped off the sidewalk and into the ooze.
Next thing I knew, I stepped out of my shoes!

Mud on my ankles and mud on my clothes.
I stumbled face-first and got mud up my nose.
Spring will be pretty, but I must confess,
The first days of spring are a muckety mess!

Dave Crawley

Hide-and-Seek

I have a perfect hiding place.
They'll never find me here.
The branches cover up my face,
So I can disappear.

I know that I will not be found.
I like the place I chose—
Although this soggy, sloggy ground
Is soaking through my clothes.

This sticker bush is prickling me,
And I don't like these ants.
I hate the way they're tickling me
While crawling up my pants.

The seekers won't give up the chase.
They'll search all afternoon.
I have a perfect hiding place.
I hope they find me soon!

Dave Crawley

I Love Summer—Except

I love all the fun
That summertime brings—
Excepting, of course
Just one or two things:
Except for the ticks
And spiders and bees.
Except for the pollen
From grasses and trees.
Except for the sunburn
And rashes from heat
And sidewalks so hot
They burn up my feet.
Except for sour grapes
And melons with seeds
And slithery snakes
That hide in the weeds.
Except for mosquitoes
That suck on my skin,
And all of the flies
That let themselves in.
Except for the fish
That I never caught,
Except for the weather
That's humid and hot.
Except for the smog,
The dust, and the grime—

But other than that,
I love summertime.

Janice Kuharski

Cannonball

The lifeguard won't let me go back in the pool.
He tells me I've broken his number one rule.
He didn't approve of my summertime smash—
The Sultan of Soakers, the cannonball splash.

The cannonball calls for an uncommon flair;
With legs tucked beneath me, I soared through the air.
With a splash that would make me the talk of the school,
I think that I just about emptied the pool.

I splashed Mr. Meese and his silly new hat.
I splashed Mrs. Simpkins, who called me a brat.
I splashed Suzy Smith from her head to her feet,
And even the lifeguard, whose whistle went *tweet*!

So now here I sit in the heat of the day.
No running. No splashing. And no way to play.
My friends are all swimming and staying real cool,
But the lifeguard won't let me go back in the pool.

Dave Crawley

The Discombobulator

Many an amusement park will boast a coaster greater,
But I have ridden each and every sluggish imitator,
And my experience confirms no solid indicator
That any ride comes even close to the Discombobulator.

It's normal to be nervous as they start to strap you in.
And if you're not, you should be, for it binds up to your chin
With safety belts and padded bars before it can begin.
Then with a screeching, jolting jerk it slowly starts to spin.

In swooshing, swelling circles it will swiftly gather speed,
Reaching such amazing heights, your nose may start to bleed,
Twisting through dark tunnels like a thundering stampede,
Then plunging down so sharply that you'll think you may have peed.

Down and down a drop that hurls you under the equator,
Your stomach hovers at the top, resigned to join you later.
Your cheeks blow back into your ears; you need a respirator.
But, oh, such pride if you survive the Discombobulator!

Lynne Hockley

Dirty Socks

My socks were very dirty,
so I washed them in the lake.
It wasn't long before I knew
I'd made a big mistake.

The water changed from clear to mud.
Then fumes began to rise.
And soon a cloud of air pollution
covered up the skies.

When bullfrogs started croaking
and ducks began to quack,
some campers started chanting,
"We want our clean lake back."

I've got a pile of dirty socks.
I'm in an awful bind.
I guess I'll have to bury them.
I hope the worms don't mind.

Bruce Lansky

My Snowman

My snowman had a lemon nose
And lemons for his ears.
His eyes were made of lemon slices,
Hair of lemon spears.

His teeth were candy lemon drops
That smiled in the shade,
But then the sun came out and turned him
Into lemonade.

Neal Levin

Snowball

I made myself a snowball
As perfect as could be.
I thought I'd keep it as a pet
And let it sleep with me.
I made it some pajamas
And a pillow for its head.
Then last night it ran away,
But first—it wet the bed.

Shel Silverstein

Critters

Sharing Showers

I shared my shower with a bug.
It loved my new shampoo—
the kind that smells like flowers
mixed with lime and honeydew.
It jumped inside the bottle,
and it swam around a bit,
and then it slowly climbed on out
to dry off and to sit.
And when the bug looked up at me
he blushed from head to toes,
embarrassed 'cuz I saw him
when he wasn't wearing clothes!

Kathy Kenney-Marshall

76

Wiggly Willy Worm

Wiggly Willy crawled along
the railroad track one day,
but when the 9:05 roared by
poor Will was in the way.

He didn't hear the warning blast,
that poor unlucky beast!
Now half of Willy's heading west;
the other's heading east.

Marilyn Helmer

Cows in the Kitchen

I'd never seen cows in the kitchen.
That's why it was such a surprise
when I went to grandmother's dairy farm,
the cows there made so many pies.

Bruce Lansky

78

The Gate

The cows are in the corn field.
The horse is in the hay.
The pigs are in the pantry,
Where I think they plan to stay.

The goose has found the grain bin
A perfect place to dine.
The goat is eating clothing
That is hanging on the line.

They're having quite a party,
But I cannot relate.
Mom stood me in the corner—
I forgot to close the gate.

Dave Crawley

Animal Appliance

The anteater has a long hose for a nose
that sucks up fat termites and ants.
I'm sure I could put one to really good use
in my bedroom, if given the chance.
I'd suck up my crayons, my checkers and socks,
my puzzles and paper and glue.
And if it had super-strong suctioning strength,
I'd suck up my big brother, too.

Andrea Perry

Tinkle, Tinkle, Little Bat

Tinkle, tinkle, little bat,
Wonders where the potty's at.

Straight ahead or to the right?
Caves are very dark at night.

Little bat, why do you frown?
Did you tinkle upside down?

Dianne Rowley

There's a Trunk up in Our Attic

There's a trunk up in our attic,
And it's been up there for years.
My parents say apparently
It's not as it appears.

There's a trunk up in our attic,
And there's one thing I can prove:
This trunk up in our attic
Is impossible to move.

There's a trunk up in our attic,
But despite what I was hopin',
It's incredibly impossible
To get the darn thing open.

There's a trunk up in our attic,
But I can't get it unlatched,
Because this trunk up in our attic
Has an elephant attached.

Neal Levin

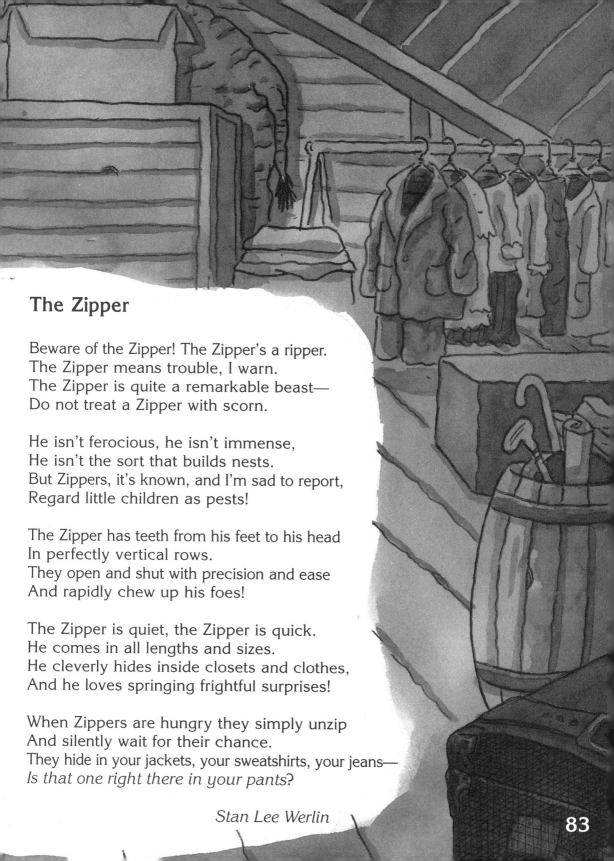

The Zipper

Beware of the Zipper! The Zipper's a ripper.
The Zipper means trouble, I warn.
The Zipper is quite a remarkable beast—
Do not treat a Zipper with scorn.

He isn't ferocious, he isn't immense,
He isn't the sort that builds nests.
But Zippers, it's known, and I'm sad to report,
Regard little children as pests!

The Zipper has teeth from his feet to his head
In perfectly vertical rows.
They open and shut with precision and ease
And rapidly chew up his foes!

The Zipper is quiet, the Zipper is quick.
He comes in all lengths and sizes.
He cleverly hides inside closets and clothes,
And he loves springing frightful surprises!

When Zippers are hungry they simply unzip
And silently wait for their chance.
They hide in your jackets, your sweatshirts, your jeans—
Is that one right there in your pants?

Stan Lee Werlin

83

Watermelon Bird

In mid-July, my friends and I
were drinking lemonade
and eating watermelon
in the comfort of the shade.
We spat the seeds among the weeds.
We spat them east and west.
I spat one in a pine tree, where
it landed in a nest.

And there it lay till late in May,
when it sprouted as a vine,
and soon there grew a melon
in the branches of the pine.
A mother bird without a word
then settled in the tree
and nested on that melon
for a week or maybe three.

A day ago, I stood below
and heard an awful scratching:
the picking and the pecking
of that watermelon hatching.
Then very soon that afternoon,
a feathered head broke free,
and now a giant baby bird
is sitting in our tree.

He's green and red from tail to head.
His eyes are small and gray.
He likely weighs a hundred pounds
and will not go away.
So be on guard in your backyard
when in the shade you sit.
Enjoy the watermelon,
but be careful where you spit.

Eric Ode

Mother Goose

Fleas as White as Snow

Mary had a little lamb,
Little lamb, little lamb.
Mary had a little lamb
With fleas as white as snow.

And everywhere that Mary went,
Mary went, Mary went,
Everywhere that Mary went,
Those fleas were sure to go.

They followed her to school one day,
School one day, school one day.
They followed her to school one day
In time for show-and-tell.

They made the children scratch away,
Scratch away, scratch away.
They made the children scratch away,
And Mary got expelled.

Neal Levin

Blow Your Nose!

Little Boy Blue,
please blow your nose.
It drips like a faucet
and sprays like a hose.
Your brother and sister
are getting upset,
so please blow your nose
'cause you're getting them wet!

Bruce Lansky

Georgie Porgie

Georgie Porgie, pudding and pie,
Kissed the girls and made them cry.
His bad breath drove the girls away.
Now he gargles twice a day.

Mark Benthall

Little Miss Muffet

Little Miss Muffet
sat on a tuffet,
eating her curds and whey.

Along came a spider
she swallowed inside her,
and that's where he is to this day.

Linda Knaus

Prank Call

Humpty Dumpty

Humpty Dumpty sat on a wall.
Humpty Dumpty had a great fall.
Humpty's lawyer filed a suit,
Now he's an egg with a lot of loot.

Mark Benthall

Humpty Dumpty sat on a wall.
Humpty Dumpty made a prank call.
Now all the king's horses
and all the king's men
won't answer the phone
if he calls them again.

Linda Knaus

Silly Stuff

Shelley Sellers

Shelley Sellers sells her shells
at Shelley's Seashell Cellars.
She sells shells (and she sure sells!)
to smelly seashore dwellers.

Smelly dwellers shop the sales
at Shelley's seashell store.
Salty sailors stop their ships
for seashells by the shore.

Shelley's shop—a shabby shack
so sandy, salty, smelly—
still sells shells despite the smells;
a swell shell shop for Shelley.

Kenn Nesbitt

The Silly Square Dance

Round we go, do-si-do.
Swing your partner to and fro.
Pull her hair, kick his shins.
Now is when the fun begins.

Do-si-do into place.
Push a mud pie in her face.
Spray her with a water hose.
Clamp a clothespin on his nose.

Swing your partner by the middle.
Throw tomatoes at the fiddle.
Promenade across the floor.
Fling your partner out the door.

Do-si-do and squash a cake.
Scare your lady with a snake.
Trip your man, stomp his feet—
silly square dance now complete.

Helen Ksypka

How Many Doofuses Does It Take to Screw In a Light Bulb?

One to bring the hammer,
One to start the drill,
One to haul the ladder,
One to hold it still.
One to buy a light bulb,
One to drop and break it,
One to buy another,
One to stop and shake it.
One to say: "It's good!"
One to say: "It's not!"
One to stop the argument.
One to mark the spot.

One to call the neighbor,
One to lend the wrench,
One to wash the ceiling,
One to move the bench.
One to build a scaffold,
One to test its strength,
One to measure height,
One to measure length.
One to bring the iodine,
One to call the doc,
One to flick the switch—
And one to take the shock.

Gary Turchin

Never

Never hide a snake inside
Your bottom dresser drawer.
Never take a Twinkie from
The corner grocery store.
Never bring a pig to school
To share for show-and-tell.
Never reach the classroom half
An hour past the bell.
Never play the tuba when
Your father's sleeping in.
Never do a somersault
In church—it is a sin.

Never dig up flowers from
Your mother's flower bed.
Never tell your sister that
Her favorite fish is dead.
Never glue a marble in
Your babysitter's shoe.
Never do, in fact, the things
That little children do.
(Well, maybe just a few.)

Joyce Armor

Don't Touch the Ice Cream

I thought I was doing a wonderful job,
Cleaning up after my dog, Cooper.
But my father got mad and said I was bad
For using his ice-cream scooper.

Darren Sardelli

Today Was Not My Day at All

Today was not my day at all,
today was not my day,
for everything went wrong today
in almost every way.
This morning I was menaced
by a troop of marching ants,
I brushed my teeth with shaving cream,
I split my brand-new pants.

I smashed my only glasses,
and the key snapped in the lock,
the toaster didn't toast the toast,
then handed me a shock.
I walked into a doorknob,
something squirmed inside my shoe,
I found an ugly beetle
at the bottom of my stew.

A bird I didn't recognize
flew down and pecked my nose,
a chimpanzee on roller skates
sped by and squashed my toes.
I wonder if I'm under
some unlucky sort of curse,
today's the twelfth, and Thursday—
tomorrow may be worse.

Jack Prelutsky

I'm Practically Covered with Needles and Pins

I'm practically covered with needles and pins,
a teakettle's firmly affixed to my shins,
my ankles are clanking with clippers and keys,
and several spoons are attached to my knees.

The fork on my forehead is making me frown,
the bolts on my shoulders are weighing me down,
a jingle bell's ringing right under my nose,
and tacks add a finishing touch to my toes.

A hook is adhering to each of my ears,
my head is topped off by a mountain of gears,
my waist is encircled by washers and wheels,
and hinges are holding on fast to my heels.

My back is embellished with ladles and chain,
the saw on my stomach's becoming a pain,
my neck is adorned with a stainless-steel pen—
I doubt that I'll swallow a magnet again.

Jack Prelutsky

Holidays

Another Note from Mom

I sprang from bed and bumped my head and stubbed my little toe,
then jammed my fingers turning down the blaring radio.

I rubbed my bumps and bruises as the weather lady said,
"Today's the first of April, look for showers overhead."

I trudged downstairs to breakfast, where my bad luck tagged along.
There taped up to the microwave...another note from Mom:

Good morning! Exclamation point—she always starts out nice.
Now comes the part where I get fed her motherly advice.

*For breakfast, dear, just help yourself. There's pizza in the fridge.
And as for soda, choose the Sprite—the Coke has lost its fizz.*

"Is this a dream?" I said out loud. "There must be some mistake.
I'd better read that through again. I'm only half awake."

I scanned the lines, not once, but twice. Yes, *pizza*'s what it said!
And I could swallow that advice, so I read on ahead:

Please wear your faded jeans to school, those low-cut ones that flare.
And use my mousse to do that sticky-up thing with your hair.

"Is she for real?" I asked myself. What's gotten into Mom?
Whatever it was, I liked it lots, so I continued on:

About your science quiz today—the one on natural gas—
Just tell your teacher that's one subject you don't want to pass!

I know I didn't read that right. I couldn't have, no way!
But there it was in black and white, as plain as night and day.

And then it hit me, why the change: Mom hadn't lost a screw;
My worry-free philosophy had finally gotten through.

Her rules had changed from lame to lax—my mom was cool at last!
These last few months of middle school were gonna be a blast!

I quickly read the last few lines: *Enjoy your day at school!*
(And don't believe what you've just read…or you're an April Fool!)

Diane Z. Shore

My Secret List for Halloween

Last year I made a secret list
Of houses on our street
That gave out all the very best
Of what I like to eat.

I made a separate list of those
That gave out candy bars
And those that let us pick right from
Their giant candy jars.

I checked off all the houses that
Gave raisins in a box
And those that gave just one
    small piece
Of gum that's hard as rocks.

My little sister laughs at me,
But I don't think she's funny,
'Cause she won't let me see her list
Of houses that gave money!

Charles Ghigna

Scary Costume

With an evil eye that stares you down
and a bulbous warty nose,
a furrowed brow, a nasty scowl,
and old outdated clothes,
my costume is the scariest
the world has ever seen.
I'm not an ogre, ghost, or ghoul:
I'm a teacher for Halloween.

Robert Pottle

The Haunting

Witches, goblins, ghosts, and ghouls go creeping through the night.
Headless riders gallop by; a truly haunting sight.

From the nearby woods you hear a wolfman's eerie howl.
Bogeymen and skeletons and vampires on the prowl.

If these creatures frighten you, I pray you'll heed my warning.
Avoid the scariest sight of all: my sister in the morning.

Tom Shadley

103

Christmas Dinner

Fruitcake.
Candied yams.
Mincemeat.
Roasted hams.
Eggnog.
Turkey legs.
Aspic.
Deviled eggs.
Gravy.
Dinner rolls.
Take some.
Pass the bowls.

Jell-O.
Christmas punch.
Cookies.
Munch, munch, munch.
Stuffing.
Gingerbread.
Whoops, I'm
overfed!
After
such a load,
feel like
I'll explode.
Guess I'm
gonna die,
so please
pass the pie.

Kenn Nesbitt

105

No Cookies for Santa

It's Christmas morning,
And I'm feeling sick.
I forgot to leave cookies
And milk for St. Nick.

But he didn't mind
'Cause his note just said,

Great!
I hope that this
Christmas
I finally lose
weight!

Charles Ghigna

Credits

The publisher has made every effort to trace ownership of the copyrighted material contained in this anthology and to secure all necessary permission to reprint. In the event that any acknowledgment has been inadvertently omitted, we express our regrets and will make all necessary corrections in future printings.

Grateful acknowledgment is made to the following for permission to publish the copyrighted material listed below:

Joyce Armor for "Never." Copyright © 2004 by Joyce Armor. Used by permission of the author.

Mark Benthall for "Georgie Porgie," "Humpty Dumpty," and "My Goldfish." Copyright © 2004 by Mark Benthall. Used by permission of the author.

Blue Lobster Press for "Magic Show" and "Scary Costume" from *MOXIE DAY and Family* by Robert Pottle. Copyright © 2002 by Robert Pottle. Used with permission from Blue Lobster Press.

Nancy Jean Clemens for "Oh, Brother!" Copyright © 2004 by Nancy Jean Clemens. Used by permission of the author.

Christopher Cook for "Benjie Poffenroth." Copyright © 2004 by Christopher Cook. Used by permission of the author.

Dave Crawley for "Cannonball," "The Gate," "Hide-and-Seek," and "Spring Will Be Pretty." Copyright © 2004 by Dave Crawley. Used by permission of the author.

Ann Dorer for "Not True." Copyright © 2004 by Ann Dorer. Used by permission of the author.

Harcourt, Inc. for "School Lunch" from *Laugh-eteria*. Copyright ©1999 by Douglas Florian. Reprinted with permission of Harcourt, Inc.

Matthew M. Fredericks for "Fraidy Cat." Copyright © 2004 by Matthew M. Fredericks. Used by permission of the author.

Charles Ghigna for "My Secret List for Halloween," from *Halloween Night: Twenty-One Spooktacular Poems*, published by Running Press; and "No Cookies for Santa." Copyright © 2004 by Charles Ghigna. Used by permission of the author.

HarperCollins Publishers for "I'm Practically Covered with Needles and Pins" from *A Pizza the Size of the Sun* by Jack Prelutsky, text copyright © 1996 by Jack Prelutsky; and "My First Best Friend" and "Today Was Not My Day at All" from *It's Raining Pigs and Noodles* by Jack Prelutsky, text copyright © 2000 by Jack Prelutsky. Used by permission of HarperCollins Publishers.

HarperCollins Publishers for "Little Abigail and the Beautiful Pony" from *A Light in the Attic*, text copyright © 1981 by Evil Eye Music, Inc.; and "Snowball" from *Falling Up*, copyright © 1996 by Shel Silverstein. Used by permission of HarperCollins Publishers.

Trevor Harvey for "Vac" and "What I'd Like to Ask My Grandma." Copyright © 2004 by Trevor Harvey. Used by permission of the author.

Marilyn Helmer for "Wiggly Willy Worm." Copyright © 2004 by Marilyn Helmer. Used by permission of the author.

Lynne Hockley for "The Discombobulator." Copyright © 2004 by Lynne Hockley. Used by permission of the author.

Kathy Kenney-Marshall for "The Favorite," "Insomnia," "My Normal Family," "Open House," and "Sharing Showers." Copyright © 2004 by Kathy Kenney-Marshall. Used by permission of the author.

Linda Knaus for "Favorite Feature," "Little Miss Muffet," "My Brother Bart," "Now I Lay Me Down to Rest," and "Prank Call." Copyright © 2004 by Linda Knaus. Used by permission of the author.

Linda Knaus and Kenn Nesbitt for "Meat Loaf" and "Willie's Wart." Copyright © 2004 by Linda Knaus and Kenn Nesbitt. Used by permission of the authors.

Helen Ksypka for "The Silly Square Dance" and "Uncle Alfonso's Hair." Copyright © 2004 by Helen Ksypka. Used by permission of the author.

Janice Kuharski for "I Love Summer—Except." Copyright © 2004 by Janice Kuharski. Used by permission of the author.

Bruce Lansky for "Blow Your Nose!" "Cows in the Kitchen," "Dirty Socks," "Mind Your Manners," and "My Dog Has Got No Manners," copyright © 2000 by Bruce Lansky, first published in *If Pigs Could Fly...and Other Deep Thoughts*; and "My Brother's Bear," copyright © 2002 by Bruce Lansky, first published in *Funny Little Poems for Funny Little People*. Used by permission of the author.

Neal Levin for "Afterschool Snack," "Baby Ate a Microchip," "Daddy's Nails," "Fleas as White as Snow," "My Snowman," and "There's a Trunk up in Our Attic." Copyright © 2004 by Neal Levin. Used by permission of the author.

Angela Magnan for "Mommy's Jewelry." Copyright © 2004 by Angela Magnan. Used by permission of the author.

Judith Natelli McLaughlin for "I Brushed My Teeth Each Morning." Copyright © 2004 by Judith Natelli McLaughlin. Used by permission of the author.

Mary Jane Mitchell for "Curing the Hiccups." Copyright © 2004 by Mary Jane Mitchell. Used by permission of the author.

Jeff Mondak for "Daddy's Making Dinner." Copyright © 2004 by Jeff Mondak. Used by permission of the author.

Kenn Nesbitt for "Christmas Dinner," "I Bought My Mom an Apple," "My Dog Likes to Disco," and "Shelley Sellers." Copyright © 2004 by Kenn Nesbitt. Used by permission of the author.

Kimberly Norman for "Mirror, Mirror o'er the Sink." Copyright © 2004 by Kimberly Norman. Used by permission of the author.

Eric Ode for "Cat and Mouse," "Rules for the Bus," and "Watermelon Bird." Copyright © 2004 by Eric Ode. Used by permission of the author.

Andrea Perry for "Animal Appliance." Copyright © 2004 by Andrea Perry. Used by permission of the author.

A. Maria Plover for "My Brother Fred" and "It Can't Be Time to Take a Bath." Copyright © 2004 by A. Maria Plover. Used by permission of the author.

Dianne Rowley for "Tinkle, Tinkle, Little Bat." Copyright © 2004 by Dianne Rowley. Used by permission of the author.

Darren Sardelli for "Don't Forget to Share" and "Don't Touch the Ice Cream." Copyright © 2004 by Darren Sardelli. Used by permission of the author.

Ted Scheu for "Foul Mouth," "Lost and Found," and "My Parents Are Pretending." Copyright © 2004 by Ted Scheu. Used by permission of the author.

Amy S. Mullins for "Love Struck." Copyright © 2004 by Amy S. Mullins. Used by permission of the author.

Tom Shadley for "Dog Hollywood" and "The Haunting." Copyright © 2004 by Tom Shadley. Used by permission of the author.

Diane Z. Shore for "Another Note from Mom." Copyright © 2004 by Diane Z. Shore. Used by permission of the author.

Timothy Tocher for "Excuse Cheer." Copyright © 2004 by Timothy Tocher. Used by permission of the author.

Gary Turchin for "How Many Doofuses Does It Take to Screw In a Light Bulb?" Copyright © 2004 by Gary Turchin. Used by permission of the author.

Stan Lee Werlin for "The Zipper." Copyright © 2004 by Stan Lee Werlin. Used by permission of the author.

Author Index

Title Index

Also from Meadowbrook Press

✦ **The Aliens Have Landed!**
Author Kenn Nesbitt, a brilliant new star in the poetry galaxy, writes with the rhythmic genius of Jack Prelutsky and the humor of Bruce Lansky. Children will love the imaginative world of Kenn Nesbitt, a world with mashed potatoes on the ceiling, skunks falling in love, antigravity machines, and aliens invading the school—all wonderfully brought to life in illustrations by Margeaux Lucas.

✦ **A Bad Case of the Giggles**
Be prepared to hear chuckles, chortles, hoots, and hollers when kids discover this anthology of funny poems…it will leave them with "a bad case of the giggles."

✦ **Kids Pick the Funniest Poems**
Three hundred elementary-school kids will tell you that this book contains the funniest poems for kids—because they picked them! Not surprisingly, they chose many of the funniest poems ever written by favorites like Shel Silverstein, Jack Prelutsky, Jeff Moss, and Judith Viorst (plus poems by lesser-known writers that are just as funny). This book is guaranteed to please children ages 6–12!

✦ **If Kids Ruled the School**
Guaranteed to make you giggle, grin, and guffaw, this anthology is brimming with side-splitting poetry. Touching on subjects from homework, tests and grades, show-and-tell, and falling asleep in class, to school lunches, awkward moments, bad hair, and the ups and downs experienced by every student in school.

✦ **No More Homework! No More Tests!**
A hilarious collection of poems about school by the most popular children's poets, including Shel Silverstein, Jack Prelutsky, Bruce Lansky, David L. Harrison, Colin McNaughton, Kalli Dakos, and others who know how to find humor in any subject.

✦ **Miles of Smiles**
The third book in Bruce Lansky's highly successful series of humorous children's poetry anthologies.

For more poetry fun, check out
www.gigglepoetry.com!

We offer many more titles written to delight, inform, and entertain.
To order books with a credit card or browse our full
selection of titles, visit our website at:

www.meadowbrookpress.com

or call toll-free to place an order, request a free catalog, or ask a question:

1-800-338-2232

Meadowbrook Press • 5451 Smetana Drive • Minnetonka, MN • 55343